The Sound of Silents

QUOTES FROM THE COMEDY STARS OF THE SILVER SCREEN

★ ★ ★

DAVE RICHARDSON

"I'M NEVER GETTING
MARRIED AGAIN,
I'M JUST GOING TO FIND
A WOMAN I DON'T LIKE
AND BUY HER A HOUSE"
STAN LAUREL

"THE SILENT PICTURE IS A UNIVERSAL MEANS OF EXPRESSION"
CHARLIE CHAPLIN

ART DIRECTION Dave Richardson DESIGN Julia Kennedy
Special thanks to John Parkin
Copyright ©Dave Richardson/Perennial Music/PlayDigital 2019

"I AM A CITIZEN
OF THE WORLD"

"MY ATTIRE IS A CONTRADICTION: THE PANTS BAGGY, THE COAT TIGHT, THE HAT SMALL AND THE SHOES LARGE"

CHARLIE CHAPLIN

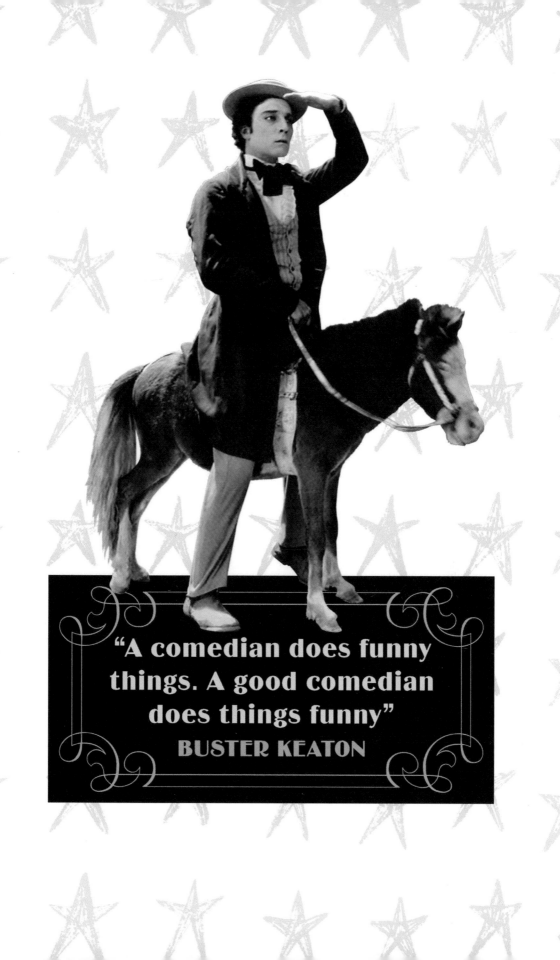

"A comedian does funny things. A good comedian does things funny"
BUSTER KEATON

"THIS IS A RUTHLESS
WORLD AND ONE
MUST BE RUTHLESS
TO COPE WITH IT"

CHARLIE CHAPLIN

"I am just turning 40 and taking my time about it" HAROLD LLOYD

"A friend once asked me what comedy was. That floored me. What is comedy? I don't know. Does anybody? Can you define it? All I know is I learned how to get laughs, and that's all I know about it. You have to learn what people will laugh at, and proceed accordingly"

STAN LAUREL

"ALL I NEED TO MAKE A COMEDY IS A PARK, A POLICEMAN AND A PRETTY GIRL"

CHARLIE CHAPLIN

"A comedian should establish a character with human appeal. Then he'll be pretty indestructible. For instance, in developing my character I use little childish gestures – and children are always appealing. Such a comedian isn't a machine. I know the limits of my character – a little too aggressive for instance, and he's gone. I've tried to inject this character into parts offered me, but if the director interfered the character would be lost"
HARRY LANGDON

"A knick-knack is the thing that sits on a whatnot" OLLIE

LAUREL & HARDY

"The first thing I did in the studio was to want to tear that camera to pieces. I had to know how that film got into the cutting room, what you did to it there, how you projected it, how you finally got the picture together, how you made things match. The technical part of the pictures is what interested me. Material was the last thing in the world I thought about. You only had to turn me loose on the set and I'd have material in two minutes, because I'd been doing it all my life"

BUSTER KEATON

" Stan I hear the ocean is infatuated with sharks " OLLIE

LAUREL & HARDY

"I'M BEN TURPIN AND
I EARN $3000 A WEEK"

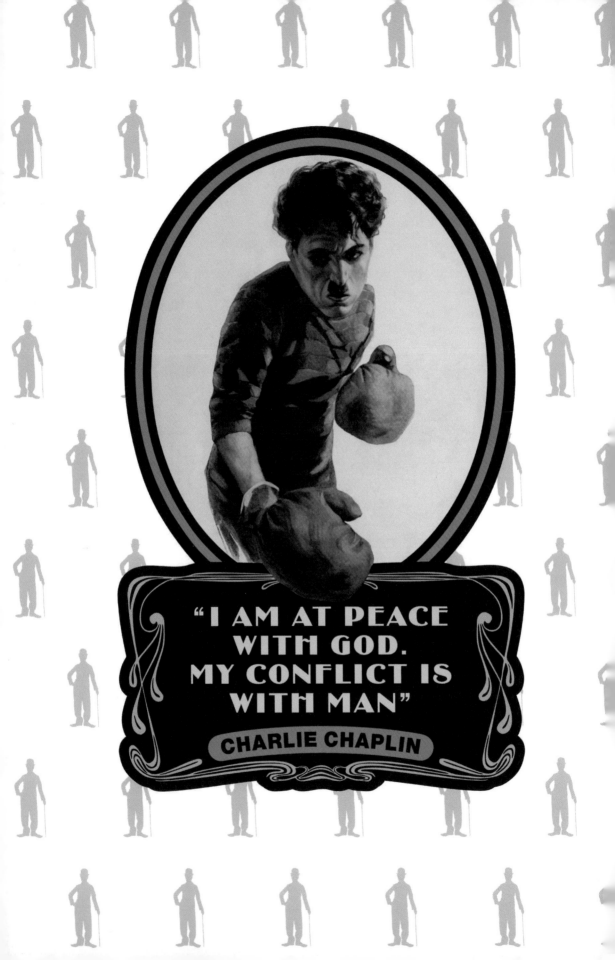

"I AM AT PEACE
WITH GOD.
MY CONFLICT IS
WITH MAN"

CHARLIE CHAPLIN

"I DON'T FEEL QUALIFIED TO TALK ABOUT MY WORK"
BUSTER KEATON

"Septober, Octember,
no wonder" STAN

LAUREL & HARDY

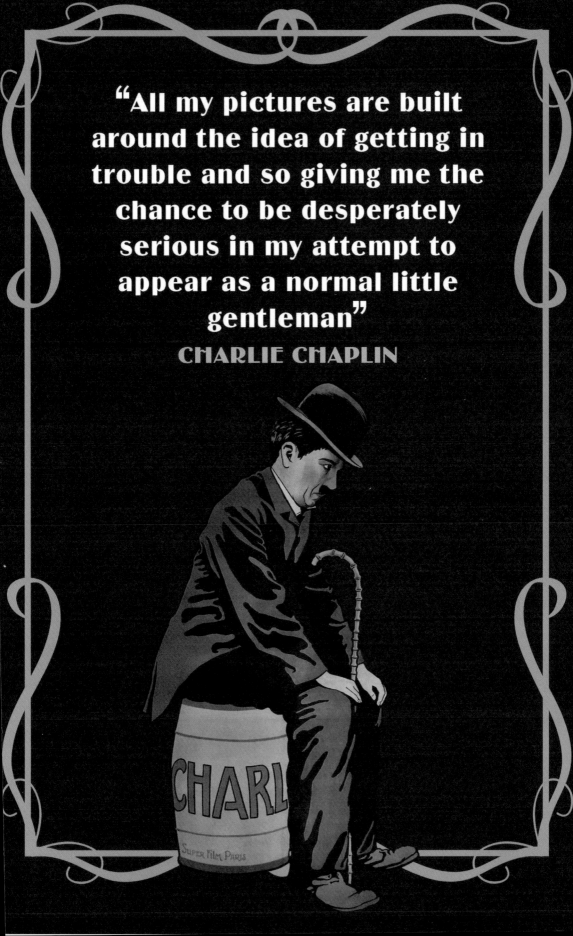

"All my pictures are built around the idea of getting in trouble and so giving me the chance to be desperately serious in my attempt to appear as a normal little gentleman"

CHARLIE CHAPLIN

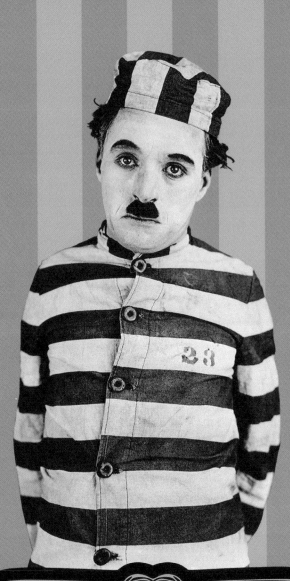

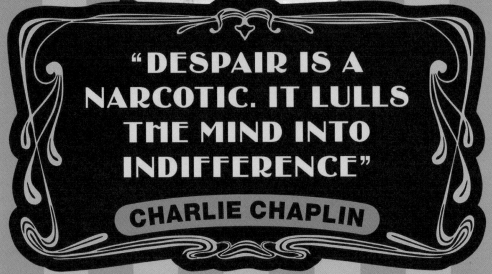

"DESPAIR IS A NARCOTIC. IT LULLS THE MIND INTO INDIFFERENCE"

CHARLIE CHAPLIN

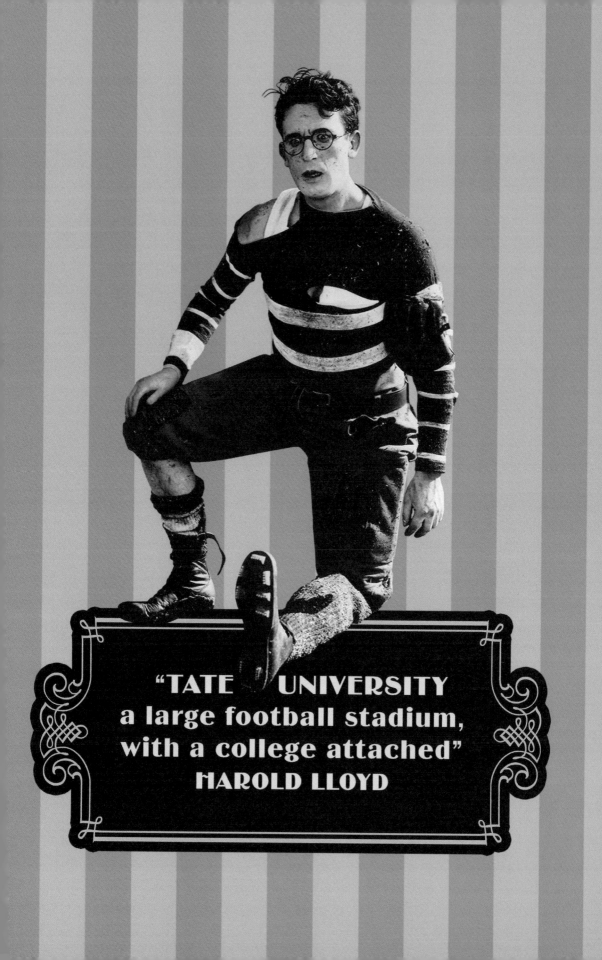

"TATE UNIVERSITY a large football stadium, with a college attached" HAROLD LLOYD

"Why didn't you tell me you had two legs" OLLIE "Well, you didn't ask me – I've always had them" STAN

LAUREL & HARDY

"MOVIES ARE A FAD.
AUDIENCES REALLY
WANT TO SEE LIVE
ACTORS ON A STAGE"

CHARLIE CHAPLIN

"LANGDON WAS EVEN GREATER THAN CHAPLIN, BUT BECAUSE HE WAS SO SIMPLE, HE NEVER UNDERSTOOD WHY HE WAS GREATER" FRANK CAPRA

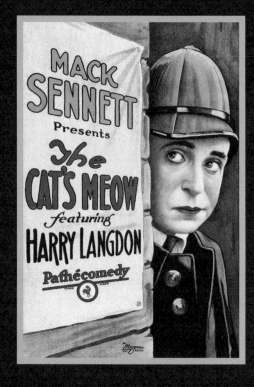

"MY MOTTO IS:
THROW YOURSELF INTO
THE GAME AND TRUST
IN PROVIDENCE"
BEN TURPIN

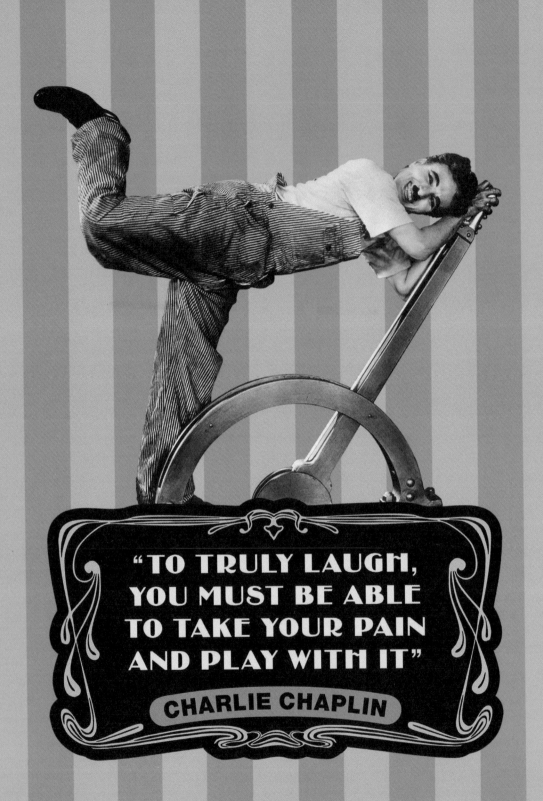

"TO TRULY LAUGH, YOU MUST BE ABLE TO TAKE YOUR PAIN AND PLAY WITH IT"

CHARLIE CHAPLIN

"Anyone who thinks 'Modern Times' has got a big message is just putting it there himself. Charlie knew that the pressures of modern life and factory life would be good for a lot of laughs, and that's why he did the film – not because he wanted to diagnose the industrial revolution"

STAN LAUREL

"Down through the years my face has been called a sour puss, a dead pan, a frozen face, The Great Stone Face, and, believe it or not, 'a tragic mask.' On the other hand that kindly critic, the late James Agee, described my face as ranking 'almost with Lincoln's as an early American archetype, it was haunting, handsome, almost beautiful.' I can't imagine what the great rail splitter's reaction would have been to this, though I sure was pleased"

BUSTER KEATON

"You're actually using your brain. That's what comes of associating with me" OLLIE

LAUREL & HARDY

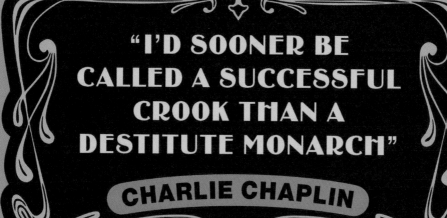

"I'D SOONER BE
CALLED A SUCCESSFUL
CROOK THAN A
DESTITUTE MONARCH"

CHARLIE CHAPLIN

"Well Stanley, when you're the biggest dog on the porch, no one will care how loud you bark!" OLLIE

LAUREL & HARDY

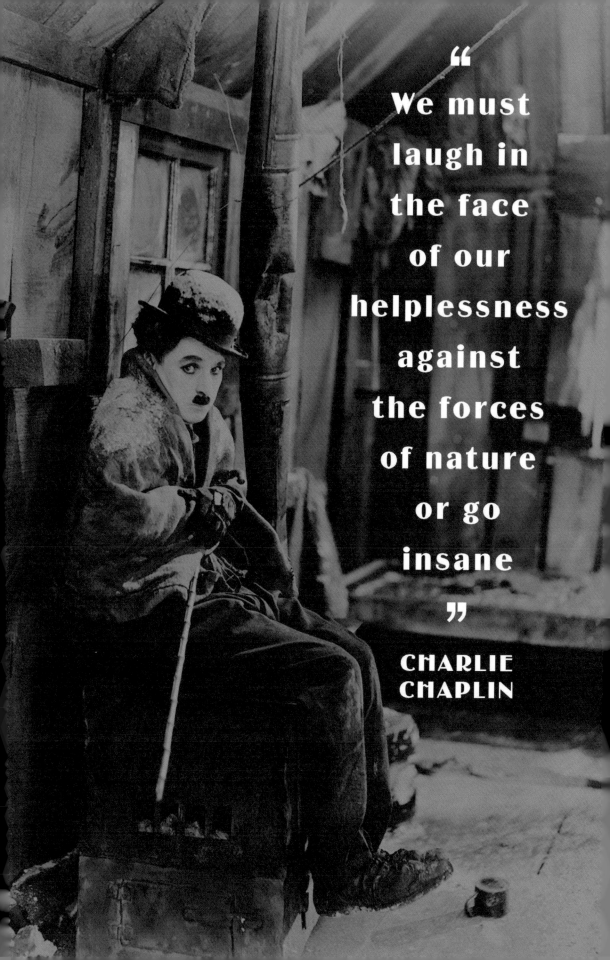

"
We must
laugh in
the face
of our
helplessness
against
the forces
of nature
or go
insane
"

CHARLIE
CHAPLIN

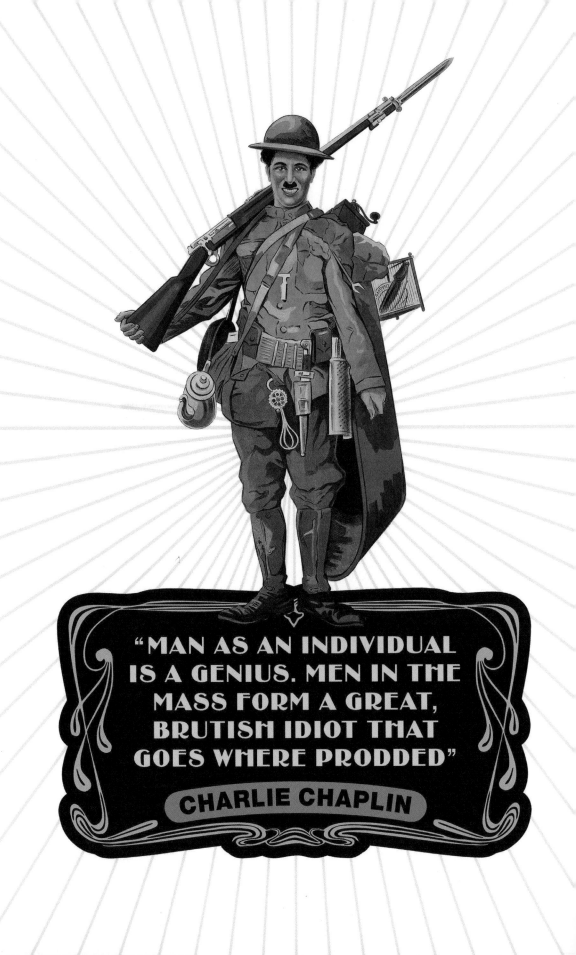

"MAN AS AN INDIVIDUAL IS A GENIUS. MEN IN THE MASS FORM A GREAT, BRUTISH IDIOT THAT GOES WHERE PRODDED"

CHARLIE CHAPLIN

"All I know is how to make people laugh" STAN

LAUREL & HARDY

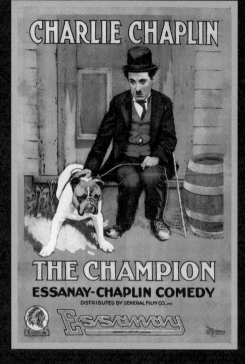

"WHAT A SAD BUSINESS, BEING FUNNY" CHARLIE CHAPLIN

"IN MY OPINION BEN TURPIN IS ONE OF THE REALLY GOOD COMEDIANS IN MOTION PICTURES"
CHARLIE CHAPLIN

"Is Hollywood the cruelest city in the world? Well, it can be"
BUSTER KEATON

"LIFE COULD BE WONDERFUL IF PEOPLE WOULD LEAVE YOU ALONE"

CHARLIE CHAPLIN

"Dreamboat ... that's what she'll say when she sees me" OLLIE
"When I see you, I think tugboat" STAN

LAUREL & HARDY

> **That is why, no matter how desperate the predicament is, I am always very much in earnest about clutching my cane, straightening my derby hat and fixing my tie, even though I have just landed on my head**
>
> **CHARLIE CHAPLIN**

HARRY LANGDON

"Women have a keener sense of humor than men, are more observing and responsive. Women care more for comedy than men do, too. You have to get dirty to get men to laugh"

"NOTHING IS PERMANENT IN THIS WICKED WORLD - NOT EVEN OUR TROUBLES"

CHARLIE CHAPLIN

"You know there's a right and wrong way to do everything" OLLIE

LAUREL & HARDY

"And if there is sweeter music this side of heaven I haven't heard it"
BUSTER KEATON

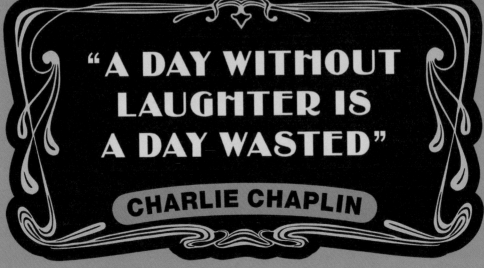

"A DAY WITHOUT LAUGHTER IS A DAY WASTED"

CHARLIE CHAPLIN

STAN

"Do you mind if I have another idea?"

OLLIE

"If it's anything like the last one, yes"

"Humor is the truth, wit is an exaggeration of the truth" STAN

LAUREL & HARDY

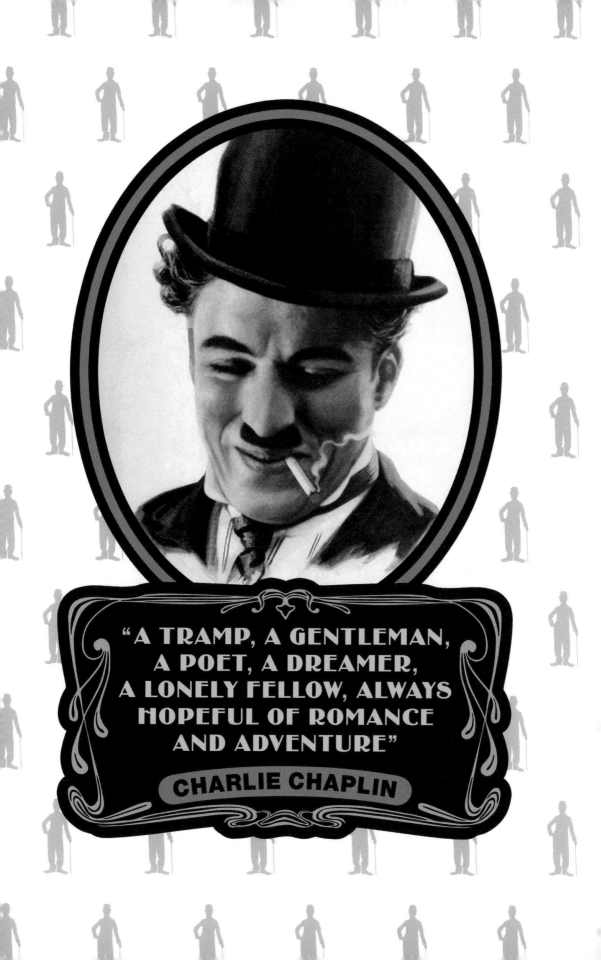

"A TRAMP, A GENTLEMAN, A POET, A DREAMER, A LONELY FELLOW, ALWAYS HOPEFUL OF ROMANCE AND ADVENTURE"

CHARLIE CHAPLIN

"Don't keep doing that.
You sound like a seal" OLLIE

LAUREL & HARDY

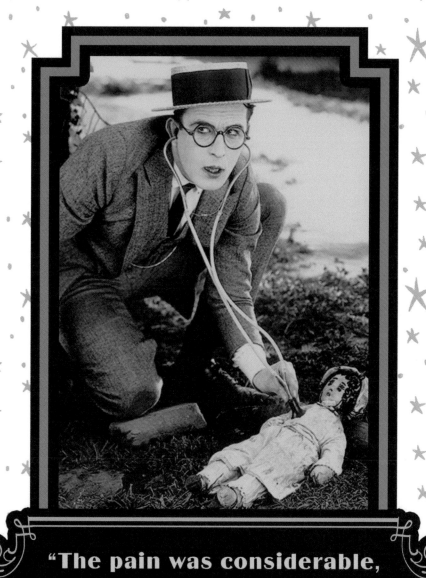

"The pain was considerable, but trivial compared with my mental state" HAROLD LLOYD

"A MAN'S TRUE CHARACTER COMES OUT WHEN HE'S DRUNK"

CHARLIE CHAPLIN

> "If one more person tells me this is just like old times, I swear I'll jump out of the window"

BUSTER KEATON

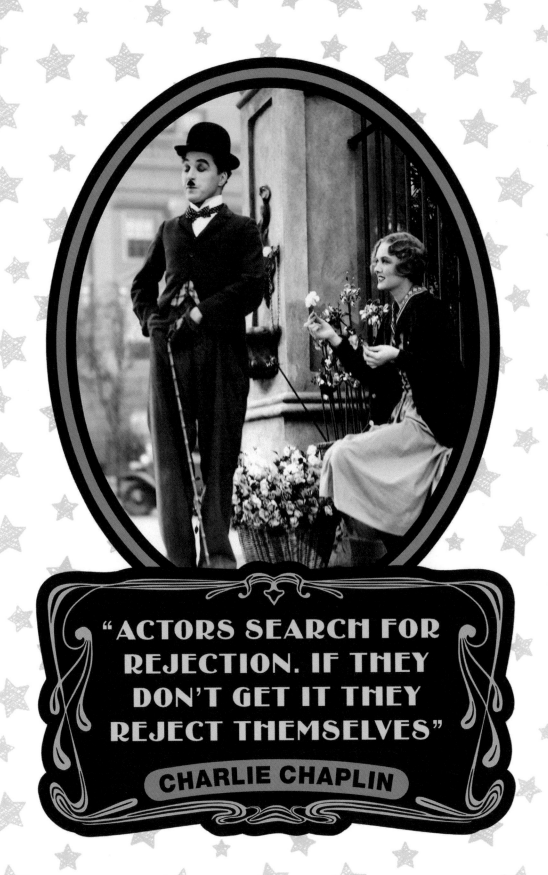

"ACTORS SEARCH FOR REJECTION. IF THEY DON'T GET IT THEY REJECT THEMSELVES"

CHARLIE CHAPLIN

"You can lead a horse to water, but a pencil must be led" STAN

LAUREL & HARDY

"LAUGHTER IS THE TONIC, THE RELIEF, THE SURCEASE FOR PAIN"

CHARLIE CHAPLIN

"I gotta do some sad scenes. Why. I never tried to make anybody cry in my life! And I go 'round all the time dolled up in hippie clothes, wear everything but a corset, can't stub my toe in this picture nor anything! Just imagine having to play-act all the time without ever getting hit with anything!"

BUSTER KEATON

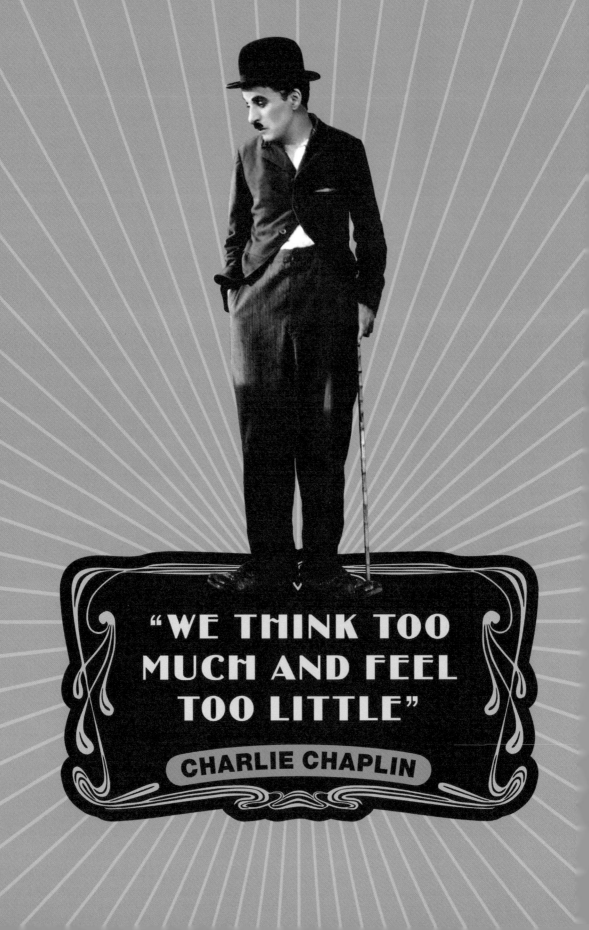

"WE THINK TOO MUCH AND FEEL TOO LITTLE"

CHARLIE CHAPLIN

"Where there's
a will, there's a way"
OLLIE

LAUREL & HARDY

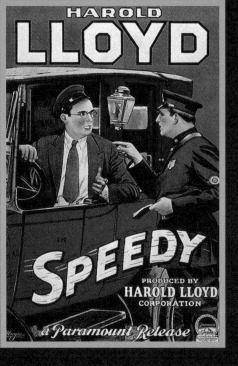

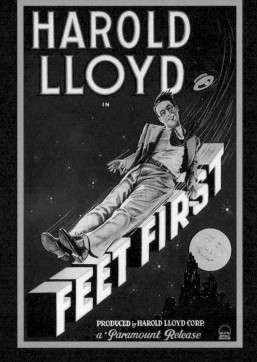

"MY HUMOR WAS NEVER CRUEL OR CYNICAL, I JUST TOOK LIFE AND POKED FUN AT IT" HAROLD LLOYD

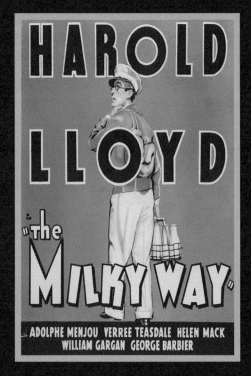

"NEVER LET YOUR
RIGHT EYE KNOW WHAT
YOUR LEFT EYE IS DOING"
BEN TURPIN

"If any of you cry at my funeral I'll never speak to you again" STAN

LAUREL & HARDY

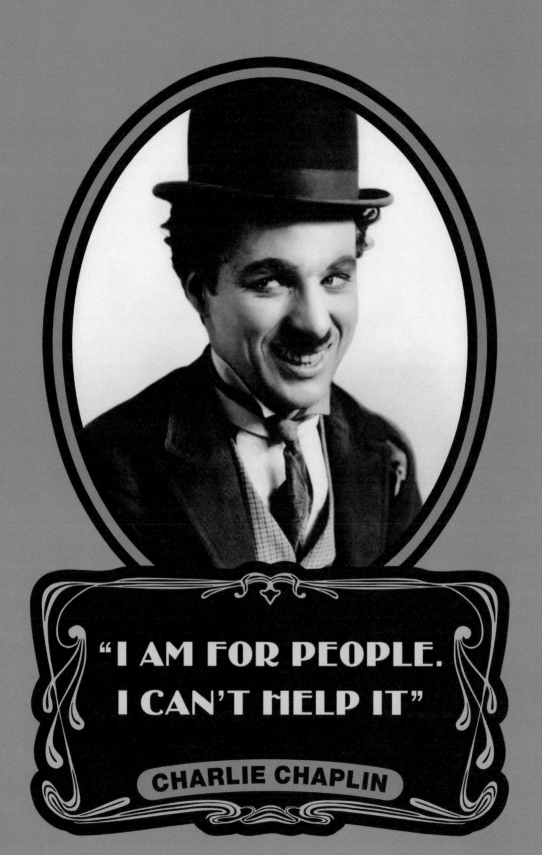

"I AM FOR PEOPLE.
I CAN'T HELP IT"

CHARLIE CHAPLIN

"The oddest thing about all
this funny-business is that
the public really wants to
laugh, but it's the hardest
thing to make them do it"
HARRY LANGDON

"On the trail of
the lonesome pine"

LAUREL & HARDY

"FAILURE IS UNIMPORTANT. IT TAKES COURAGE TO MAKE A FOOL OF YOURSELF"

CHARLIE CHAPLIN

"I don't deserve
to be mentioned in the
same sentence with
Charles Chaplin"
STAN LAUREL

"YOU'LL NEVER FIND RAINBOWS LOOKING DOWN"

CHARLIE CHAPLIN

"No man can be a genius in slap shoes and a flat hat"

BUSTER KEATON

"I CAN DO EIGHT DIFFERENT KINDS OF FALLS AND THEY'RE ALL REAL, BELIEVE ME" BEN TURPIN

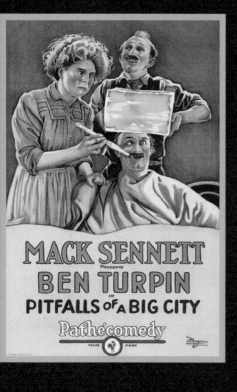

"DICTATORS FREE
THEMSELVES
BUT THEY ENSLAVE
THE PEOPLE"

CHARLIE CHAPLIN

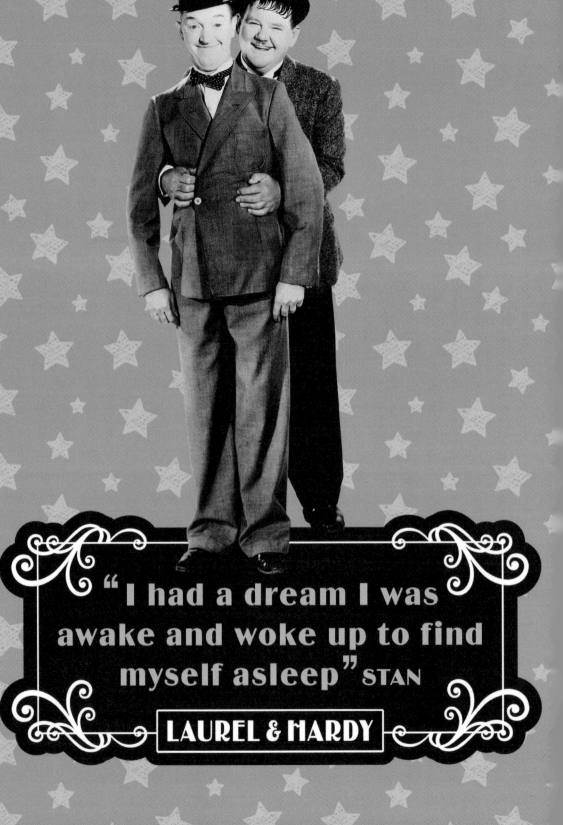

" I had a dream I was awake and woke up to find myself asleep " STAN

LAUREL & HARDY

"We all want to help one another. Human beings are like that. We want to live by each other's happiness, not by each other's misery"

CHARLIE CHAPLIN

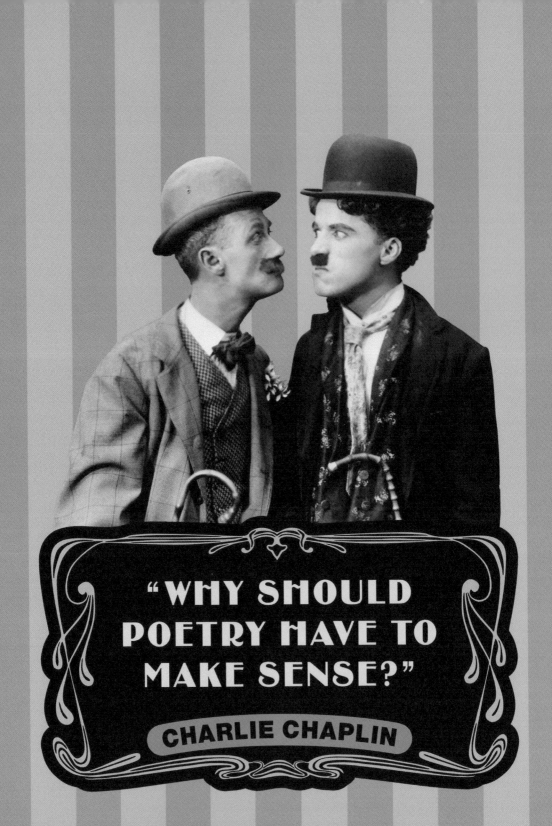

"WHY SHOULD POETRY HAVE TO MAKE SENSE?"

CHARLIE CHAPLIN

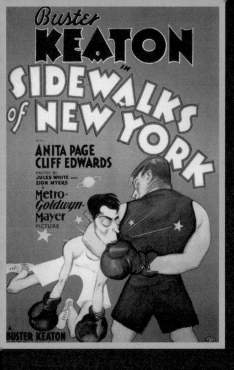

"SILENCE IS OF THE GODS, ONLY MONKEYS CHATTER" BUSTER KEATON

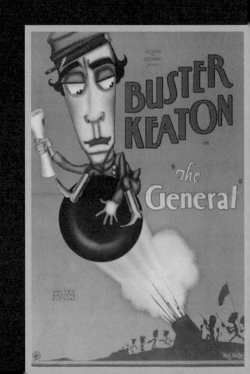

"BEN TURPIN IS RISING
FAST AS A COMEDIAN.
HIS WORK IS NATURAL"
CHARLES H. RYAN

"Your bark is worse than your over-bite" STAN

LAUREL & HARDY

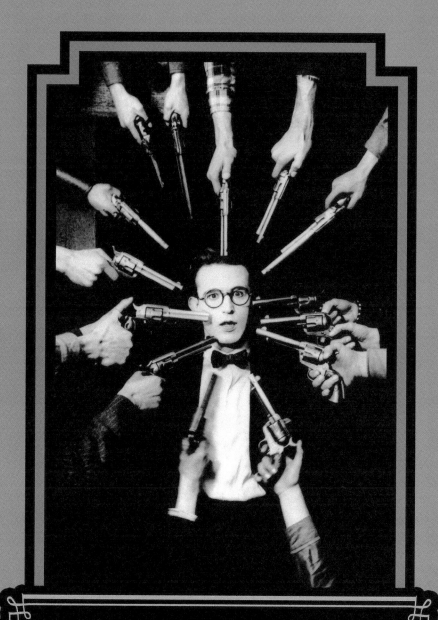

"The more trouble you get a man into, the more comedy you get out of him"
HAROLD LLOYD

"If you had a face like mine, you'd punch me right on the nose, and I'm just the fella to do it" STAN

LAUREL & HARDY

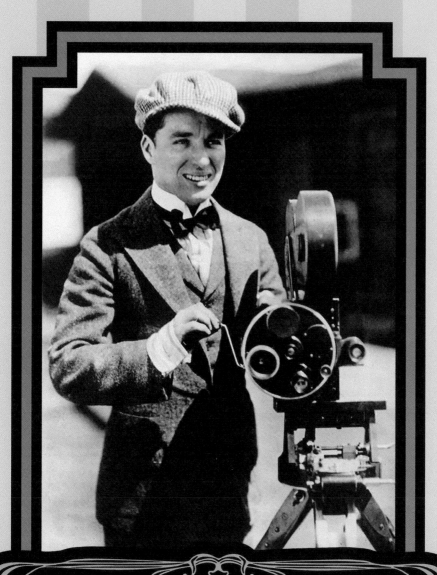

"LIFE IS A TRAGEDY
WHEN SEEN IN CLOSE-UP,
BUT A COMEDY IN
LONG-SHOT"

CHARLIE CHAPLIN

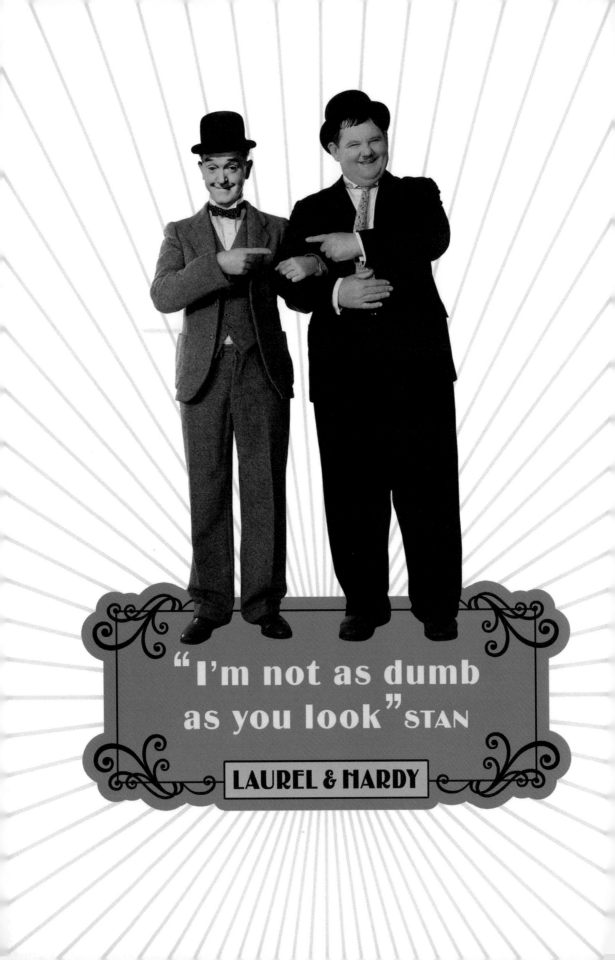

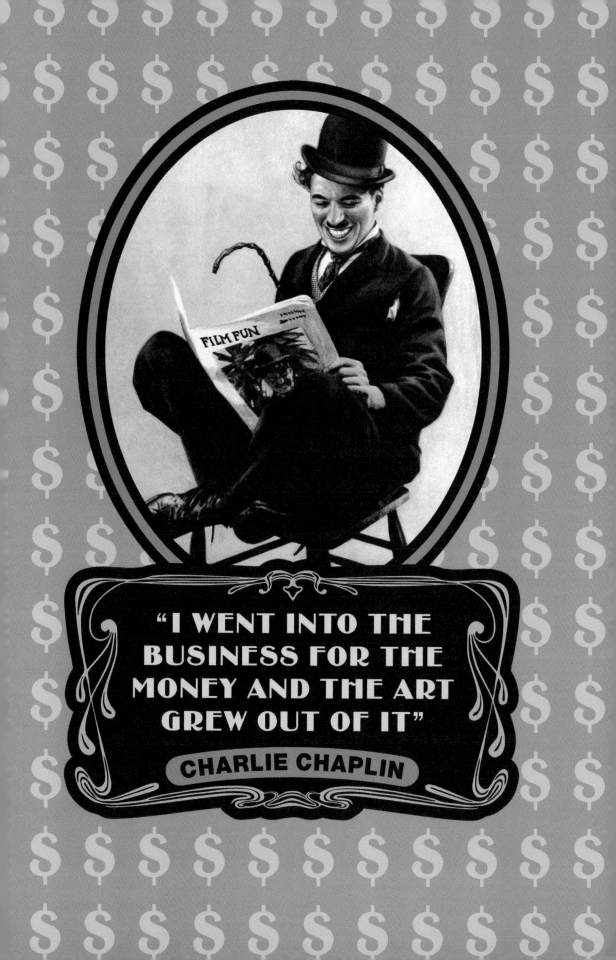

"I WENT INTO THE BUSINESS FOR THE MONEY AND THE ART GREW OUT OF IT"

CHARLIE CHAPLIN

"All my life I've been happiest when folks watching me said to each other, 'Look at the poor dope, wilya?'"
BUSTER KEATON

"THE SADDEST
THING I CAN
IMAGINE IS TO GET
USED TO LUXURY"

CHARLIE CHAPLIN

OLLIE: "What do you mean you don't know what my letter said? You just read it to me"
STAN: "I know Ollie, but it was private, so I didn't listen"

LAUREL & HARDY

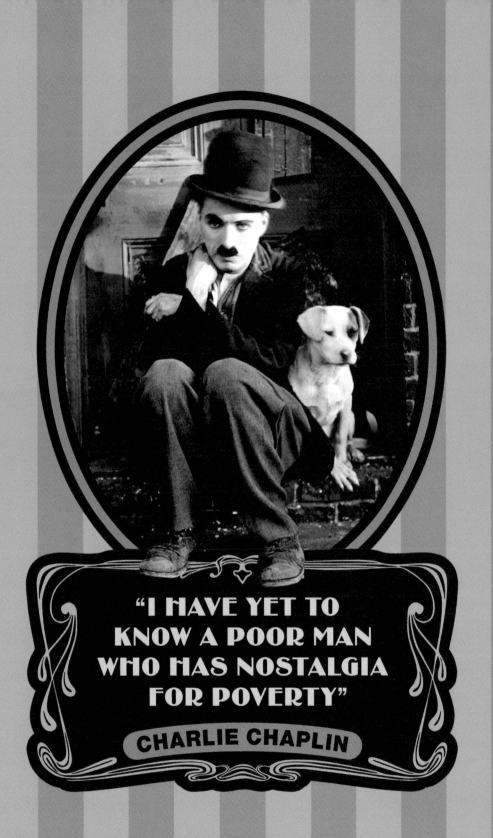

"I HAVE YET TO KNOW A POOR MAN WHO HAS NOSTALGIA FOR POVERTY"

CHARLIE CHAPLIN

"PEOPLE HAVE ALWAYS LOVED OUR MOVIES, I GUESS THAT'S BECAUSE THEY SAW HOW MUCH LOVE WE PUT INTO THEM" STAN LAUREL

"LAUGH AND THEY
HAND YOU THE HA-HA;
WEEP AND THEY GREET
YOU WITH THE HEE-HEE"
BEN TURPIN

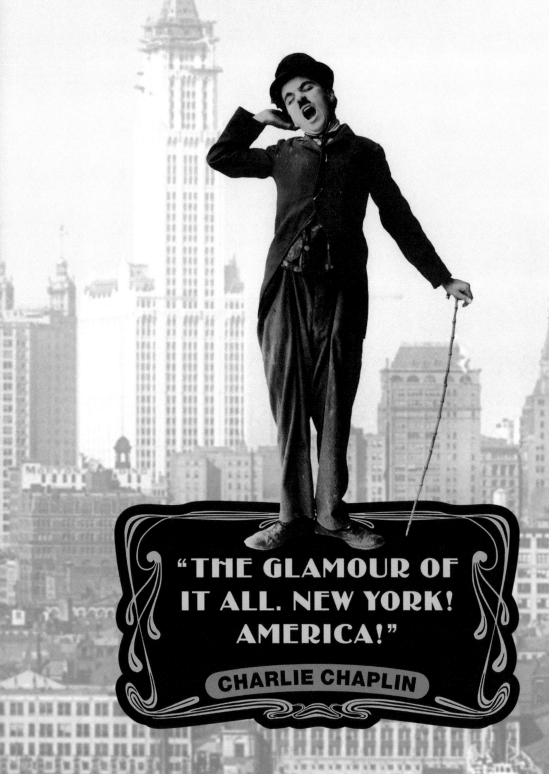

"THE GLAMOUR OF IT ALL. NEW YORK! AMERICA!"

CHARLIE CHAPLIN

HARRY LANGDON

"Without character, a comedian is lost.
When I play in what I call the O-OUCH-O
comedies, where the comedian runs about,
is hit on the head, etc, I am just an
animated suit of clothes"

"ONLY THE UNLOVED HATE; THE UNLOVED AND THE UNNATURAL"

CHARLIE CHAPLIN

"The man who tries
to be funny is lost"
HAROLD LLOYD

OLLIE: "Bring me a parfait"
STAN: "Put one on my steak too"

LAUREL & HARDY

"Not long ago a friend asked me what was the greatest pleasure I got from spending my whole life as an actor. There have been so many that I had to think about that for a moment. Then I said, like everyone else, I like to be with a happy crowd"

BUSTER KEATON

"I SUPPOSE THAT'S ONE OF THE IRONIES OF LIFE DOING THE WRONG THING AT THE RIGHT MOMENT"

CHARLIE CHAPLIN

" IT'S MY FACE WOT MAKES MY CLOTHES LOOK SHABBY!! "

STAN LAUREL

"WORDS ARE CHEAP.
THE BIGGEST
THING YOU CAN SAY
IS 'ELEPHANT'"

CHARLIE CHAPLIN

"Tragedy is a close-up;
comedy, a long shot"
BUSTER KEATON

"Sight gags had to be planned; they required timing and mechanics. Occasionally, spontaneity would arise in the shooting of the scenes"
STAN LAUREL

LAUREL AND HARDY
MAGICIANS

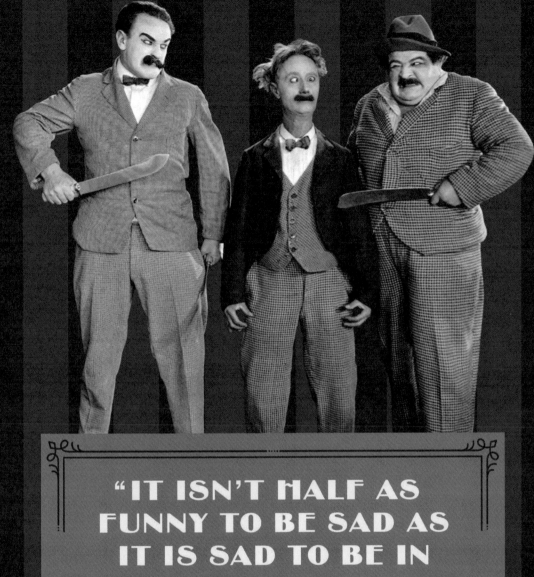

"IT ISN'T HALF AS
FUNNY TO BE SAD AS
IT IS SAD TO BE IN
THE COMEDIES"
BEN TURPIN

OLLIE
"Why did you get a veterinarian?"
STAN
"Well I didn't think his religion would
make any difference"

LAUREL & HARDY

"IN THE END,
EVERYTHING
IS A GAG"

CHARLIE CHAPLIN

A SELECTION OF IMAGES FEATURED IN THIS BOOK PLUS LOADS OF OTHER DESIGNS ARE AVAILABLE ON T-SHIRTS, POSTERS, PHONE CASES, CUSHIONS, MUGS, NOTEBOOKS, POSTCARDS, etc, www.redbubble.com/people/tigerdaver

MORE BOOKS FROM DAVE RICHARDSON

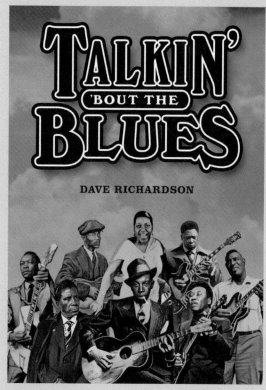

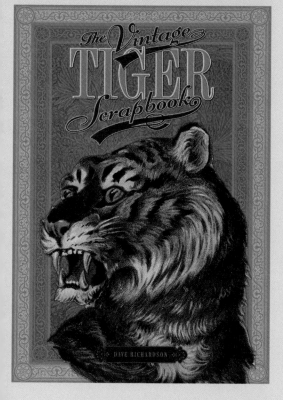

AVAILABLE AT AMAZON STORES

Printed in Poland
by Amazon Fulfillment
Poland Sp. z o.o., Wrocław